W9-CBH-524

STONY CREEK LIBRARY
1350 GREENFIELD PIKE
NOBLESVILLE, IN 46060

Learn to Draw
BACKYARD ANIMALS

MEDIA ENHANCED BOOKS

AV2 BY WEIGL™

ADDED VALUE • AUDIO VISUAL

www.av2books.com

MEDIA ENHANCED BOOKS
AV²
BY WEIGL™
ADDED VALUE • AUDIO VISUAL

Go to **www.av2books.com**, and enter this book's unique code.

BOOK CODE

R363196

AV² by Weigl brings you media enhanced books that support active learning.

AV² provides enriched content that supplements and complements this book. Weigl's AV² books strive to create inspired learning and engage young minds in a total learning experience.

Your AV² Media Enhanced books come alive with...

 Audio
Listen to sections of the book read aloud.

 Video
Watch informative video clips.

 Embedded Weblinks
Gain additional information for research.

 Try This!
Complete activities and hands-on experiments.

 Key Words
Study vocabulary, and complete a matching word activity.

 Quizzes
Test your knowledge.

 Slide Show
View images and captions, and prepare a presentation.

... and much, much more!

Published by AV² by Weigl
350 5th Avenue, 59th Floor
New York, NY 10118
Website: www.weigl.com   www.av2books.com

Copyright ©2012 AV² by Weigl.
All rights reserved. No part of this publication may be reproduced, stored in a retrieval system, or transmitted in any form or by any means, electronic, mechanical, photocopying, recording, or otherwise, without the prior written permission of the publisher.

Library of Congress Cataloging-in-Publication Data

Backyard animals / edited by Jordan McGill.
    p. cm. -- (Learn to draw)
  Includes index.
  ISBN 978-1-61690-857-7 (hardcover : alk. paper) -- ISBN 978-1-61690-863-8 (pbk. : alk. paper) -- ISBN 978-1-61690-987-1 (online)
1. Animals in art--Juvenile literature. 2. Wildlife art--Juvenile literature. 3. Drawing--Technique--Juvenile literature. I. McGill, Jordan.
  NC780.B29 2011
  743.6--dc23
                          2011020310

Printed in the United States of America in North Mankato, Minnesota
3 4 5 6 7 8 9 0 17 16 15 14 13

022013
WEP280113

Project Coordinator: Jordan McGill
Art Director: Terry Paulhus

Every reasonable effort has been made to trace ownership and to obtain permission to reprint copyright material. The publishers would be pleased to have any errors or omissions brought to their attention so that they may be corrected in subsequent printings.

Weigl acknowledges Getty Images as its primary image supplier for this title.

38888000173421

Contents

6

10

14

18

22

26

3

Why Draw?

Drawing is easier than you think. Look around you. The world is made of shapes and lines. By combining simple shapes and lines anything can be drawn. An orange is just a circle with a few details added. A flower can be a circle with ovals drawn around it. An ice cream cone can be a triangle topped with a circle. Most anything, no matter how complicated, can be broken down into simple shapes.

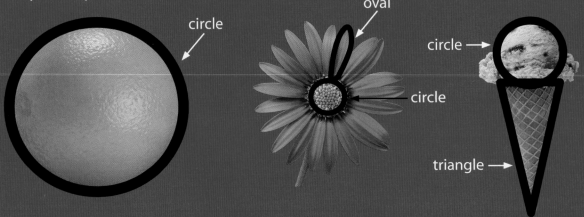

circle

oval

circle

circle

triangle

Drawing helps people make sense of the world. It is a way to reduce an object to its simplest form, say our most personal feelings and thoughts, or show others objects from our **imagination**. Drawing an object can help you learn how it fits together and works.

What shapes do you see in this car?

It is fun to put the world onto a page, but it is also a good way to learn. Learning to draw even simple objects introduces the skills needed to fully express oneself visually. Drawing is an excellent form of **communication** and improves people's imagination.

Practice drawing your favorite animals in this book to learn the basic skills necessary to draw. You can use those skills to create your own drawings.

Backyard Animals

Drawing backyard animals is a great way to learn about the different parts and features that make them adaptable and able to survive in their changing environment. As you draw each part of the animals in this book, consider how that part benefits the animal. Think about how the animal's features allow it to survive in a changing environment.

Animals live in nearly every corner of the world. Earth's human **population** grows every year. To find food and shelter, humans have started to move into regions that were once home to animals. This changes the animal's natural environment.

In cities across the United States, some animals now live near people. These animals are commonly seen by people, sometimes in their own backyards. Backyard animals are still wild, and they have **adapted** to **survive** in their environment. This can make them dangerous.

Meet the Bat

Bats are small, flying **mammals**. They are the only mammals that can fly. Bats have large wings made of two layers of skin. This skin stretches over their long finger bones and arms. It connects to the sides of the body and back legs. Their bodies are covered in fur. Bats often have black or brown fur. It can also be gray, white, red, or orange.

Bats live in nearly every part of the world, except for the North and South Poles. They eat mosquitoes and bugs to help keep neighborhoods insect-free.

Head

For their body size, bats have larger brains than birds. They are very smart. Bats can remember places and people for a long time.

Wings

Bat wings are made of skin. Bats have long finger bones that support their wings. The wings stretch from the hind leg to the fingers. Bats have a thumb that is free from the wing. They use their thumb to cling to trees and ceilings. The largest bats in the world have wingspans of up to 6 feet (1.8 meters).

Ears

Bats can turn their ears in the direction of sounds. At night, bats make small, high-pitched noises. These noises echo, or bounce off, other objects. The bats hear the echoes, which help them find **prey**. The echoes also help them avoid flying into objects.

Eyes

Bats have good eyesight. They can see well at night.

Teeth

Bats have small, sharp teeth with jagged edges. They use their teeth to break through the hard shells of fruit and prey, such as insects.

STONY CREEK LIBRARY
1350 GREENFIELD PIKE
NOBLESVILLE, IN 46060

How to Draw a
Bat

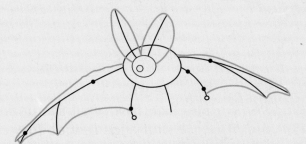

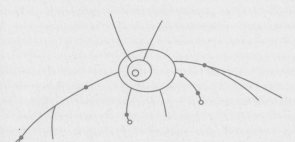

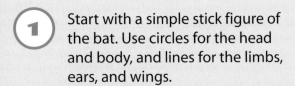

1 Start with a simple stick figure of the bat. Use circles for the head and body, and lines for the limbs, ears, and wings.

2 Now, join the two wings with the body circle using smooth, curved lines. Also, draw ovals around the lines on the head for ears.

3 Next, join the wings with the legs. This will become the web between the wings and the legs.

4 In this step, draw the legs and veins in the web of the wings, as shown.

5 Next, draw the eyes, nose, and mouth.

6 Now, draw curved lines inside the ovals for the ears.

7 Draw hair on the body and checkered lines on the wings.

8 Erase the extra lines and the stick figure frame.

9 Color the picture.

Meet the Deer

Deer are mammals. They have big eyes and sharp hearing. Deer have a good sense of smell. They can run fast, and they are good swimmers.

Male deer are called bucks. Bucks have antlers on their head. Most female deer do not have antlers. They are called does.

Deer are found in North America, Europe, northern Africa, and Asia. They live in open meadows, mountains, forests, and swamps.

Nose
A deer's sense of smell is much more sensitive than a human's. A deer's nose has **membranes** that capture scents easily.

Teeth
Deer teeth are made to chew tough food, such as plants. Deer have **incisors** that allow them to bite. **Molars** help deer grind their food into smaller pieces.

Eyes
Deer have large eyes on both sides of their head. This allows them to see in front and behind without moving their head.

Antlers

Often, only male deer grow antlers. In some species, such as caribou, both males and females grow antlers.

Ears

Deer have large ears. They can hear very well. Deer ears rotate, or turn. They pick up sounds quickly.

Coat

A deer's coat acts as **camouflage**. It is reddish-brown in the summer to blend in with the leaves on trees. It is grayish-brown in the winter, so it blends in with the bare forests.

How to Draw a Deer

1. Start with a simple stick figure of the deer. Use circles for the head and body, ovals for the snout and feet, and lines for the limbs and antlers.

2. Now, join the two body circles and the head together with a smooth, curved line.

3 Next, draw the ears and nose.

4 In this step, draw the legs, as shown.

5 Next, draw the antlers.

6 Now, draw the eyes and curved lines around the snout.

7 Draw the mane and hair around the body and tail.

8 Erase the extra lines and the stick figure frame.

9 Color the picture.

Meet the Eagle

Eagles are birds of prey. These birds hunt other animals for food. Eagles are warm-blooded animals that lay eggs. They have feathers, a beak with no teeth, and a small skeleton.

Eagles have hooked beaks, strong legs, and powerful talons that make it easy for them to hunt other animals. Sharp eyesight helps them spot their prey from high above.

Eagles live in every kind of **habitat**, including forests, wetlands, deserts, mountains, and farmlands. They can also live in towns and cities with parks.

Eyes
Eagles have bright yellow eyes. Their sharp vision helps them spot their prey from a great distance. They can see clearly during the day, but not at night.

Beak
The eagle has a large, hooked beak. It is powerful and can easily tear the flesh of prey. Eagles have no teeth.

Legs
Eagles have two legs, with short, powerful toes, and long **talons**. The sharp talons pierce the prey and help hold it firmly in place.

Wings
Eagles have strong, broad wings, so they can fly high without much effort. On average, they can fly at a speed of 31 miles (50 kilometers) per hour.

Feathers
An eagle's feathers, beak, and talons are made of keratin. Human fingernails are made of the same substance.

How to Draw an
Eagle

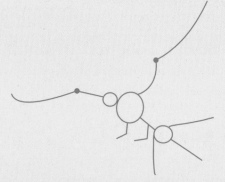

1 Start with a simple stick figure of the eagle. Use circles for the head and body, and lines for the wings, feet, and tail.

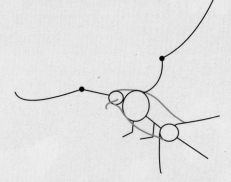

2 Now, join the head and body circles together with a smooth, curved line. Also, draw a curved line for the beak.

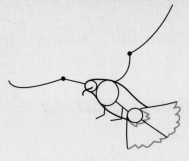

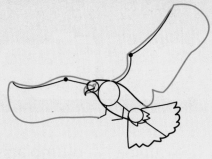

3 Next, draw two curved lines around the tail, as shown.

4 In this step, draw the beak, eye, and curved lines for the wings.

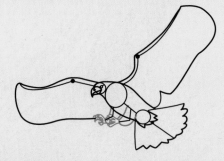

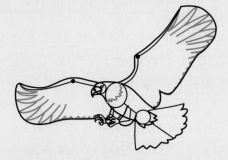

5 Next, draw the feet.

6 Now, draw feathers on the wings and body of the eagle.

7 Draw more feathers on the wings, body, and tail.

8 Erase the extra lines and the stick figure frame.

9 Color the picture.

17

Meet the Porcupine

A porcupine is a **plump** animal with a round head and thick coat. It is covered in soft hair, but it is best known for the long, pointed spikes growing from its back and sides. These are called quills, and they are sharp like needles.

Porcupines use their quills to keep them safe from **predators**. If a porcupine is **threatened** by a predator, muscles in its skin make the quills stand up on end. The porcupine then sticks some of its quills into the predator's skin if the porcupine is attacked.

Teeth
Porcupines have bright orange teeth. Their teeth are very strong. The incisors never stop growing. Porcupines use their teeth to chew tough wood and seeds.

Eyes
Porcupines have small eyes. These animals do not see well.

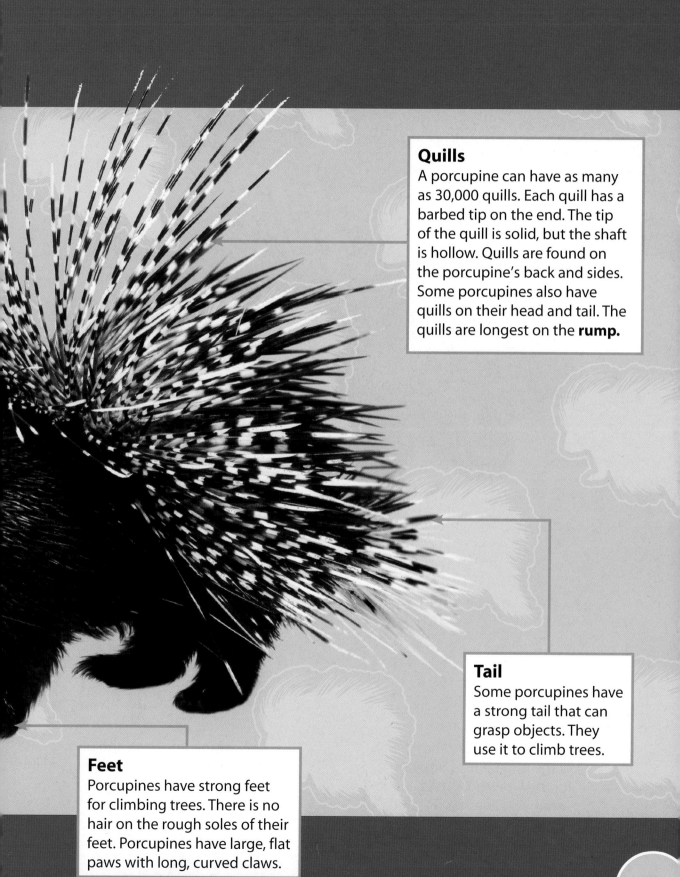

Quills

A porcupine can have as many as 30,000 quills. Each quill has a barbed tip on the end. The tip of the quill is solid, but the shaft is hollow. Quills are found on the porcupine's back and sides. Some porcupines also have quills on their head and tail. The quills are longest on the **rump.**

Tail

Some porcupines have a strong tail that can grasp objects. They use it to climb trees.

Feet

Porcupines have strong feet for climbing trees. There is no hair on the rough soles of their feet. Porcupines have large, flat paws with long, curved claws.

How to Draw a Porcupine

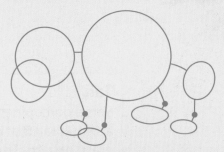

1 Start with a simple stick figure of the porcupine. Use ovals for the head, body, feet and snout, and lines for the limbs.

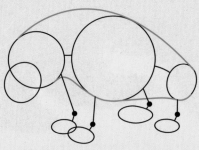

2 Now, join the head and body ovals together with a smooth, curved line.

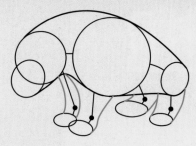

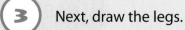

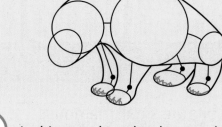

3 Next, draw the legs.

4 In this step, draw the claws, as shown.

5 Next, draw a smooth, curved line around the upper body for the quills, as shown. Also, draw the nose, eye, and ear.

6 Now, draw the quills on the upper body, inside the curved line from the previous step.

7 Draw fur on the head, body, and legs.

8 Erase the extra lines and the stick figure frame.

9 Color the picture.

Meet the Rabbit

Rabbits are small mammals that are covered with fur. They are known for their large ears and short, fluffy tail. Rabbits do not walk like other animals. They hop. They can leap 10 to 15 feet (3 to 4.5 m).

Rabbits can adapt to many places. They live in fields, meadows, farms, and even cities. Rabbits often search for food in gardens.

Nose
Rabbits have a keen sense of smell. In nature, they know other rabbits by their smell.

Teeth
Rabbits have large front teeth. They use their teeth to grip and bite plants. Rabbits' teeth are always growing. Chewing on tough bark wears down their teeth.

Ears
Rabbits have large ears that help them to hear well. Their ears can turn. This allows rabbits to hear in all directions.

Eyes
A rabbit's eyes are on either side of its head. This allows the rabbit to see a large area. Rabbits can see behind and to the side better than they can see to the front.

Fur
Rabbits can be gray, brown, black, or white. The color of their fur changes to blend in with their surroundings.

Hind Legs
Rabbits have big, strong back legs. They use their legs to hop, run, and dig tunnels. Rabbits' long legs help them move quickly. They thump their hind leg to warn other rabbits of danger.

How to Draw a Rabbit

1 Start with a simple stick figure of the rabbit. Use ovals for the head, body and feet, and lines for the limbs and tail.

2 Now, join the head and body ovals together with a smooth, curved line.

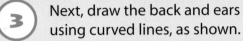

3 Next, draw the back and ears using curved lines, as shown.

4 In this step, draw the legs and feet.

5 Next, draw the toes and a curved line inside the ear.

6 Now, draw the eye, nose, and mouth.

7 Draw the whiskers, nails, and tail. Also, draw the fur on the body and face using curved lines.

8 Erase the extra lines and the stick figure frame.

9 Color the picture.

Meet the Skunk

Skunks are mammals. They have long, black and white fur with stripes, swirls, or dots. A skunk has a small head, small ears, short legs, and a long, fluffy tail. It is about the same size as a house cat.

Skunks protect themselves with their scent, or musk. When a skunk feels threatened, it warns its enemies by standing on its front legs. If its enemies do not run away, the skunk sprays them with a stinky spray. A skunk can spray up to 10 feet (3 m). This odor is hard to wash off, and it can last many days.

Eyes
Skunks cannot see well. They must rely on their sense of smell to find food.

Legs
A skunk's legs are short, so it moves slowly. Skunks waddle when they walk. Most cannot climb fences or trees because of their short legs.

Scent Glands
Scent glands under a skunk's tail make a thick, yellow, oily spray. The glands are the size of a grape. They hold enough musk for about five or six sprays. A skunk's spray can make a person ill. It can make the eyes burn, so the person or animal cannot see for a short time.

Sharp Claws
Skunks use their long, sharp claws for digging in the dirt and searching for food. Skunks eat grubs and worms that they dig out of the ground or rotting wood.

How to Draw a
Skunk

1 Start with a simple stick figure of the skunk. Use circles for the head and body, ovals for the snout and feet, and lines for the limbs and tail.

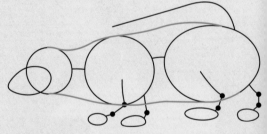

2 Now, join the head and the two body circles together with a smooth, curved line.

3 Next, draw the outline of the tail. This will be used to draw hair on the tail later.

4 In this step, draw the ear and the legs, as shown.

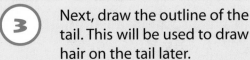

5 Next, draw the eye, nose, mouth, and feet.

6 Now, draw the fur on the tail, body, and legs. Also, draw the nails.

7 Draw more fur on the head, body, and tail.

8 Erase the extra lines and the stick figure frame.

9 Color the image.

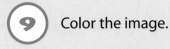

Test Your Knowledge of Backyard Animals

1.

What are the wingspans of the largest bats in the world?

Answer: 6 feet (1.8 meters)

2.

Where do deer live?

Answer: In open meadows, mountains, forests, and swamps

3.

What are an eagle's feathers, beak, and talons made of?

Answer: Keratin

4.

What color are porcupines teeth?

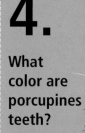

Answer: Orange

5.

How far can rabbits leap?

Answer: 10 to 15 feet (3 to 4.5 meters)

6.

How do skunks protect themselves?

Answer: With their scent, or musk

Want to learn more? Log on to av2books.com to access more content.

30

Draw an Environment

Materials
- Large white poster board
- Internet connection or library
- Pencils and crayons or markers
- Glue or tape

Steps
1. Complete one of the animal drawings in this book. Cut out the drawing.
2. Using this book and research online, or in a library, find out about your animal and the environment where it lives.
3. Think about what the animal might see and hear in its environment. What does its environment look like? What sorts of trees are there? Is there water? What does the landscape look like? Are there other animals in its environment? What in the animal's environment is essential to its survival? What other important features might you find in the animal's environment?
4. On the large white poster board, draw an environment for your animal. Be sure to place all the features you noted in step 3.
5. Place the cutout animal in its environment with glue or tape. Color the animal's environment to complete the activity.

Glossary

adapted: adjusted to the natural environment

camouflage: colors that blend in with the animal's surroundings

communication: the sending and receiving of information

habitat: natural living place

imagination: the ability to form new creative ideas or images

incisors: sharp teeth at the front of the mouth that are used for cutting

mammals: animals that have fur, make milk, and are born live

membranes: thin layers of skin tissue.

molars: teeth near the back of an animal's mouth used for grinding

plump: slightly fat

population: the number of people in an area

predators: animals that hunt and eat other animals for food

prey: animals that are hunted and eaten for food

rump: the back end of the body

survive: stay alive

talons: long nails on the claws of an eagle

threatened: to be in danger

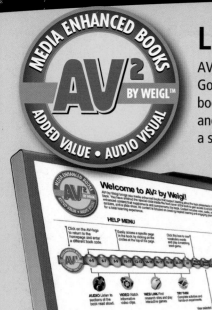

Log on to www.av2books.com

AV² by Weigl brings you media enhanced books that support active learning. Go to www.av2books.com, and enter the special code found on page 2 of this book. You will gain access to enriched and enhanced content that supplements and complements this book. Content includes video, audio, web links, quizzes, a slide show, and activities.

Audio
Listen to sections of the book read aloud.

Video
Watch informative video clips.

Embedded Weblinks
Gain additional information for research.

Try This!
Complete activities and hands-on experiments.

WHAT'S ONLINE?

Try This!	**Embedded Weblinks**	**Video**	**EXTRA FEATURES**
Complete an interactive drawing tutorial for each of the six backyard animals in the book.	Learn more about each of the six backyard animals in the book.	Watch a video about backyard animals.	

 Audio
Listen to sections of the book read aloud.

Key Words
Study vocabulary, and complete a matching word activity.

 Slide Show
View images and captions, and prepare a presentation

 Quizzes
Test your knowledge.

AV² was built to bridge the gap between print and digital. We encourage you to tell us what you like and what you want to see in the future.

Sign up to be an AV² Ambassador at www.av2books.com/ambassador.

Due to the dynamic nature of the Internet, some of the URLs and activities provided as part of AV² by Weigl may have changed or ceased to exist. AV² by Weigl accepts no responsibility for any such changes. All media enhanced books are regularly monitored to update addresses and sites in a timely manner. Contact AV² by Weigl at 1-866-649-3445 or av2books@weigl.com with any questions, comments, or feedback.